UNDERSTANDING

SIMILES

FIGURATIVELY
SPEAKING

BY
ROBIN JOHNSON

Crabtree Publishing Company
www.crabtreebooks.com

Crabtree Publishing Company

www.crabtreebooks.com

Author: Robin Johnson

Publishing plan research and development: Reagan Miller

Photo research: Margaret Amy Salter

Editorial director: Kathy Middleton

Editor: Anastasia Suen

Proofreader and indexer: Wendy Scavuzzo

Cover design and logo: Margaret Amy Salter

Layout, production coordinator and prepress technician: Margaret Amy Salter

Print coordinator: Margaret Amy Salter

Photographs:
All images by Shutterstock

Similes featured on cover:

Top: Like a bull in a china shop

Bottom left: Like looking for a needle in a haystack

Bottom right: Like water off a duck's back

Library and Archives Canada Cataloguing in Publication

Johnson, Robin (Robin R.), author
    Understanding similes / Robin Johnson.

(Figuratively speaking)
Includes index.
Issued in print and electronic formats.
ISBN 978-0-7787-1775-1 (bound).--
ISBN 978-0-7787-1875-8 (paperback).--
ISBN 978-1-4271-1616-1 (pdf).--ISBN 978-1-4271-1612-3 (html)

    1. Simile--Juvenile literature. 2. Figures of speech--Juvenile literature.
I. Title.

PN228.S5J64 2015   j808'.032   C2015-903957-6
                                    C2015-903958-4

Library of Congress Cataloging-in-Publication Data

Johnson, Robin (Robin R.)
 Understanding similes / Robin Johnson.
    pages cm. -- (Figuratively Speaking)
 Includes index.
 ISBN 978-0-7787-1775-1 (reinforced library binding) --
ISBN 978-0-7787-1875-8 (pbk.) --
ISBN 978-1-4271-1616-1 (electronic pdf) --
ISBN 978-1-4271-1612-3 (electronic html)
 1. Simile--Juvenile literature. 2. Figures of speech--Juvenile
literature. 3. English language--Terms and phrases--Juvenile
literature. I. Title.

 PE1445.S5J64 2015
 808'.032--dc23
                                      2015022592

Crabtree Publishing Company

www.crabtreebooks.com   1-800-387-7650

Printed in Canada/112015/EF20150911

Published in Canada
Crabtree Publishing
616 Welland Ave.
St. Catharines, ON
L2M 5V6

Published in the United States
Crabtree Publishing
PMB 59051
350 Fifth Avenue, 59th Floor
New York, New York 10118

Published in the United Kingdom
Crabtree Publishing
Maritime House
Basin Road North, Hove
BN41 1WR

Published in Australia
Crabtree Publishing
3 Charles Street
Coburg North
VIC, 3058

CONTENTS

Are you as cool as a cucumber? Are you and your best friend like two peas in a pod? These sentences both contain **similes**. Similes are **figures of speech** that compare two unlike things. A simile uses the words "like" or "as" to compare one thing to another.

Are you calm and cool under pressure? Cucumbers feel cool to the touch. You don't look much like a cucumber. But you and the cucumber have something in common— being cool.

You are not round and green like a pea. Peas that grow in the same pod, or case, all look the same. If you and your friend dress or act alike, then you have something in common with peas in a pod.

You could say that similes are like vegetables. Vegetables help your body grow. Similes help your stories grow! Vegetables are good for your health, and similes are good for your writing! Similes are found in all kinds of writing, from nursery rhymes to poems to novels. They are also used in everyday speech.

FIGURATIVE OR LITERAL?

We use two types of language to tell stories. We use **literal language** to state facts or describe things as they really are. We say, "Hannah was really hungry! She ate three cheeseburgers!" That is a true statement. She literally ate three burgers.

Figurative language uses words or sayings with meanings that are different from their usual, literal meanings. We say:

"Hannah ate like a horse! She had a pizza as big as the moon!"

Hannah did not really eat like a horse. She did not stand in a field and eat grass. But she did eat a lot of food, so she was similar to a horse in that way. Her pizza was not actually the size of the moon. But the simile tells us the pizza was big and round.

We use the words "like" and "as" in both literal and figurative language. But not every sentence with "like" and "as" includes a simile. It must also compare two unlike things.

LITERAL
"I like to eat bacon for breakfast."

The sentence on the left does not have a simile because it does not make a comparison. The sentence on the right includes a simile.

FIGURATIVE
"The kids ate their breakfast like pigs."

LITERAL
"My cherry pie tastes as good as your pumpkin pie."

The sentence on the left does not have a simile because it compares two things that are alike. The sentence on the right includes a simile.

FIGURATIVE
"Learning about similes is as easy as pie."

WHY USE SIMILES?

We use similes to paint pictures with words. Similes make your writing more colorful and your stories more interesting. Similes also help writers explain and describe things. They help readers understand what writers are feeling. Similes also help you picture the **characters** and **setting** in a story.

Read the sentences below. Some have similes and some do not. Spot the similes. Then compare the sentences. How do the similes help you imagine the characters and setting?

> The house was really messy.

> The house looked like a dump!

> Peter's head was as big and round as a pumpkin.

> Peter had a big, round head.

> Ashley was very tall.

> Ashley was as tall as a giraffe.

SUPERSIZED SIMILES

The similes on this page use **hyperbole**. Hyperbole is a figure of speech that **exaggerates**, or describes a thing as much better or worse than it really is. Hyperbole is used to make a point or to add humor to writing.

ABOUT THIS BOOK

This book is divided into four sections to help you make sense of similes as fast as lightning.

FIGURE IT OUT! Studies similes in different sorts of writing.

TALK ABOUT IT! Shows you how to brainstorm and use graphic organizers to start the writing process.

WRITE ABOUT IT! Includes samples and tips to help you create original work.

NOW IT'S YOUR TURN! Gets you making your own super similes in poems and stories.

FIVE STEPS TO WRITING

1. PRE-WRITING: Brainstorm new ideas. Write them all down, even if they seem as dull as dishwater.

2. DRAFTING: Your first **draft** can be as messy as a dog's breakfast—as long as you can read it.

3. REVISING: Take advice from other writers. They are like wise old owls! Then revise your work to make it even better.

4. EDITING: Read over your work. Correct any spelling or grammar mistakes. Make your work as neat as a pin.

5. PUBLISHING: Share your finished work with your friends and family, or publish it online. It's as easy as ABC!

USING SIMILES IN POEMS

Similes are perfect for poetry because most poems are short. They are made up of just a few lines. Similes help poets paint pictures with fewer words. In this poem, the poet uses "like" similes to describe his love. He paints a picture of a girl who's as pretty as a picture!

A RED, RED ROSE

O my [Love's] like a red, red rose
    That's newly sprung in June;
O my [Love's] like the melody
    That's sweetly played in tune.

—Excerpt from "A Red, Red Rose"
by Robert Burns

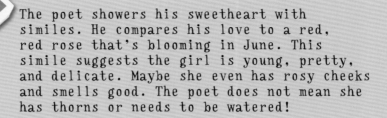

The poet showers his sweetheart with similes. He compares his love to a red, red rose that's blooming in June. This simile suggests the girl is young, pretty, and delicate. Maybe she even has rosy cheeks and smells good. The poet does not mean she has thorns or needs to be watered!

The poet also compares his love to a melody played sweetly in tune. Music makes you feel good. It makes you want to dance and twirl and jump. It makes you want to sing and hum and whistle. That is how his love makes the poet feel.

IT JUST MAKES SENSE!

Many similes rely on the five senses. They make comparisons based on how things look, smell, sound, taste, or feel. We know that a rose is beautiful and smells sweet. We also know that a melody is a pleasant sound. By comparing his love to familiar things, the poet helps the reader understand his feelings.

Madison wanted to write similes about something she loves. She decided to use her five senses to describe ice cream. Madison used a **graphic organizer** to list her ideas. In a chart, she wrote down one word that described how ice cream looks. Then she wrote a word that described how ice cream felt to the touch. She kept going until she had a word for each sense.

Then Madison thought of other things with the same **characteristics**. A characteristic is a feature or quality of a person or thing. Ice cream is cold. Madison's toes often get cold in the winter. Madison added the words "my toes in winter" to her senses chart. Then she filled in the rest of the chart.

TOPIC: Ice cream

sight	touch	 taste	sound	 smell
Ice cream looks blue	Ice cream feels cold	Ice cream tastes sweet	Ice cream sounds like drip, drip, drip	Ice cream smells like cotton candy
Another blue thing	Another cold thing	Another sweet thing	Another thing that drips	Another thing that smells like cotton candy
blueberries	my toes in winter	a jar of jellybeans	a leaky faucet	a carnival

Madison joined the words in her senses chart using "like" or "as." Then she made some sweet similes.

My scoop of ice cream looks like a big, round blueberry.

My ice cream smells like a carnival.

My melting ice cream sounds like a leaky faucet.

My ice cream tastes as sweet as a jar of jellybeans.

My ice cream feels as cold as my toes in winter.

Pick up your pen and write your own senses similes! Choose a person or thing you love. It could be your dog, bike, grandma, or anything else. Use your five senses to describe it. Does your dog bark loudly? Does your bike look shiny? Does your grandma smell sweet? Write down other things with the same characteristics. Hammering sounds loud. Nickels look shiny. Flowers smell sweet. Next, join the words together with "like" or "as" to make some comparisons.

BARK
BARK

USING SIMILES IN NURSERY RHYMES

You might not know it, but you have probably heard similes since you were a baby! Simple similes are often found in nursery rhymes. Nursery rhymes are poems and songs told to children over time. Some are as old as the hills! Can you spot the similes in these nursery rhymes?

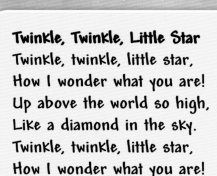

Mary Had a Little Lamb
Mary had a little lamb,
Its fleece was white as snow;
And everywhere that Mary went,
The lamb was sure to go.

Twinkle, Twinkle, Little Star
Twinkle, twinkle, little star,
How I wonder what you are!
Up above the world so high,
Like a diamond in the sky.
Twinkle, twinkle, little star,
How I wonder what you are!

In "Twinkle, Twinkle, Little Star," the little star looks like a diamond. This simile helps us picture a bright, shiny star in the sky. What if the writer had not used a simile? The nursery rhyme might have sounded like this:

> Twinkle, twinkle, little star,
> How I wonder what you are!
> Up above the world so high,
> Shining brightly in the sky.

As you can see, the simile is the star of this nursery rhyme. Without it, the poem loses some of its sparkle. It is not as interesting or fun to sing.

In "Mary Had a Little Lamb," the lamb's fleece, or wool, is white as snow. This simile helps us imagine a lamb with clean, fluffy wool. Luckily, Mary was not followed around all day by a muddy lamb! How would the poem sound without a simile?

PRETTY BAAA-D!

> Mary had a little lamb,
> Its fleece was very white;
> And everywhere that Mary went,
> The lamb went day and night.

Jacob wanted to write a nursery rhyme with a simile. He used "Mary Had a Little Lamb" as a model. Jacob's favorite animal is a snake, so he chose that as his subject. He brainstormed all the words he could think of to describe a snake and put them in a word web. Then Jacob picked one characteristic. He chose the word "big" to describe the snake in his poem.

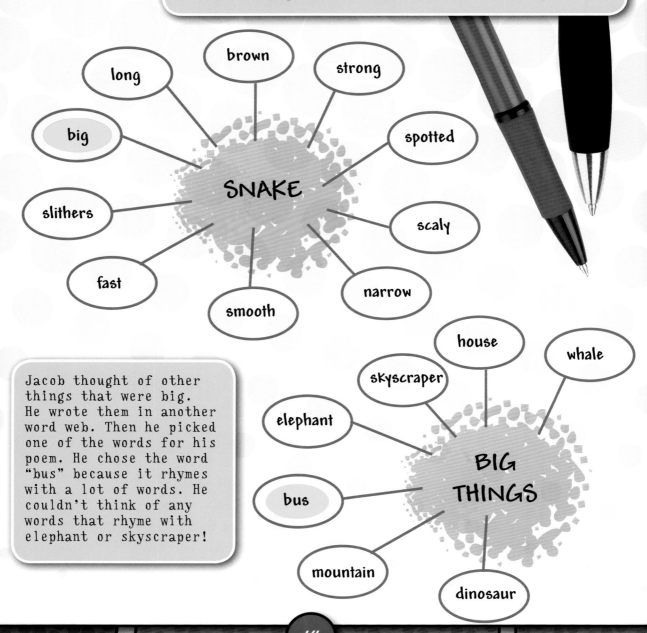

long
brown
strong

big

spotted

SNAKE

slithers

scaly

fast

narrow

smooth

Jacob thought of other things that were big. He wrote them in another word web. Then he picked one of the words for his poem. He chose the word "bus" because it rhymes with a lot of words. He couldn't think of any words that rhyme with elephant or skyscraper!

house

whale

skyscraper

elephant

BIG THINGS

bus

mountain

dinosaur

WRITE ABOUT IT!

Jacob used the words "snake," "big," and "bus" to write his nursery rhyme. He based it on "Mary Had a Little Lamb," but he changed the words to make it his own.

Jacob had a giant snake,
It was as big as a bus,
He brought the snake to class one day,
And frightened all of us!

NOW IT'S YOUR TURN!

Now it's rhyme time for you! Choose an animal. Brainstorm a list of its characteristics. Remember to use your five senses. Pick one, then think of other things with the same characteristic. Write them down. Use the words "like" or "as" to make a comparison. Then put it all together to make a nursery rhyme!

USING SIMILES IN FAIRY TALES

You have seen that similes can make poems pop. But did you know that they also paint pictures in **prose**? Prose is spoken or written words told in sentences. Prose is used in fairy tales, short stories, novels, and plays. In this chapter, you will learn about similes in fairy tales.

A fairy tale is a short children's story about magical beings and lands. It is a colorful story filled with colorful characters. Little Red Riding Hood wears a cape as red as an apple. Rapunzel has hair like spun gold. But no character is more "colorful" than Snow White.

LITTLE SNOW WHITE

Once upon a time in the middle of winter, when the flakes of snow were falling like feathers from the clouds, a Queen sat at her palace window, which had an ebony black frame, stitching her husband's shirts. While she was [busy] and looking out at the snow, she pricked her finger, and three drops of blood fell upon the snow. Now the red looked so well upon the white that she thought to herself, "Oh, that I had a child as white as this snow, as red as this blood, and as black as the wood of this frame!" Soon afterwards a little daughter came to her, who was as white as snow, and with cheeks as red as blood, and with hair as black as ebony, and from this she was named "Snow White."

—Excerpt from the fairy tale "Little Snow White"

FIGURE IT OUT!

Similes help bring characters to life. In this passage, the writer uses colorful similes to paint a picture of Snow White. Her cheeks were as red as blood. Her hair was as black as ebony, which is a dark wood. Her skin was as white as snow. Comparing Snow White to familiar things helps us imagine how she looks. We can picture her beauty. We understand why the magic mirror on the wall says she's the fairest of them all.

Similes also help develop the setting and **mood** of a story. The Queen sat at her palace window while snowflakes fell "like feathers from the clouds." Feathers are soft and light. They float gently to the ground. This simile paints a picture of a peaceful winter scene.

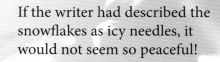

If the writer had described the snowflakes as icy needles, it would not seem so peaceful!

WHAT'S IN A NAME?
Imagine that a different simile had been used to describe Snow White. If she was white as a ghost, her name would be Ghost White. That sounds like a scary fairy tale! If she was white as a chicken, she would be called Chicken White. Maybe she would be friends with Chicken Little!

Some colorful similes are scattered throughout this book. The poet's love was like a red, red rose. Madison's ice cream scoop looked like a big blueberry. Mary's little lamb and Snow White were both as white as snow. Ella decided to come up with some colorful similes of her own.

She wrote the word "yellow" in the center of a word wheel. Then she brainstormed other words. Ella thought of all the yellow things she could. Lemons and bananas are yellow. Ducks and chicks are yellow. So are school buses and pencils. Ella wrote them all down in the word wheel. Soon her similes would be ready to roll!

HELLO, YELLOW!
Can you think of other things to add to Ella's word wheel?

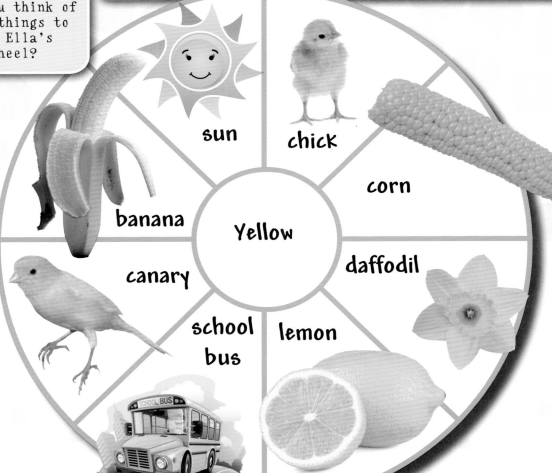

Yellow

sun

chick

corn

banana

daffodil

canary

school bus

lemon

WRITE ABOUT IT!

Ella wanted to describe some characters and objects in "Little Snow White." She used the words in her word wheel to write some colorful similes of her own.

The magic mirror shone like the sun.

The prince's hair was as soft and yellow as a chick.

The paint was as blue as the sky.

NOW IT'S YOUR TURN!

Now it's your turn to get colorful! Choose a color for the center of your word wheel. Then write down things that are that color. Get creative and show your true colors! When your wheel is full, use it to write your own colorful similes.

This boy's shirt is as green as grass.

USING SIMILES IN NOVELS

Similes are as good as gold in novels and other stories, too. Novels are long stories of fiction with characters and action. In *Treasure Island*, Robert Louis Stevenson uses seaworthy similes to set the mood for his pirate tale.

I stood straight up against the wall, my heart still going like a sledgehammer, but with a ray of hope now shining in my bosom. [Long John] Silver leant back against the wall, his arms crossed, his pipe in the corner of his mouth, as calm as though he had been in church; yet his eye kept wandering [slyly], and he kept the tail of it on his unruly followers. They, on their part, drew gradually together... and the low hiss of their whispering sounded in my ear continuously, like a stream.

—Excerpt from *Treasure Island* by Robert Louis Stevenson

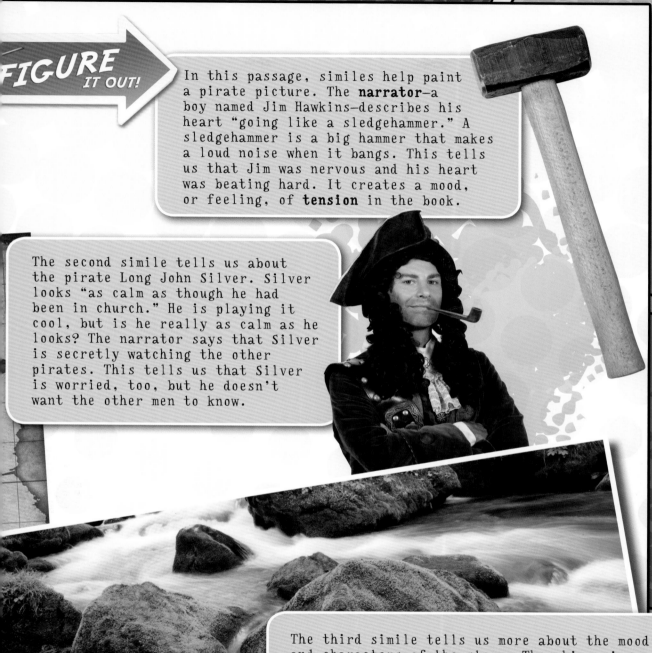

In this passage, similes help paint a pirate picture. The **narrator**—a boy named Jim Hawkins—describes his heart "going like a sledgehammer." A sledgehammer is a big hammer that makes a loud noise when it bangs. This tells us that Jim was nervous and his heart was beating hard. It creates a mood, or feeling, of **tension** in the book.

The second simile tells us about the pirate Long John Silver. Silver looks "as calm as though he had been in church." He is playing it cool, but is he really as calm as he looks? The narrator says that Silver is secretly watching the other pirates. This tells us that Silver is worried, too, but he doesn't want the other men to know.

The third simile tells us more about the mood and characters of the story. The whispering pirates sounded "like a stream." The water in a stream flows fast, so we imagine the men are talking quickly. A stream makes a steady noise, so we picture the men all speaking at once. If the pirates are whispering fast at the same time, they are probably worried, too!

Cooper wanted to practice telling stories with similes. Instead of pirates searching for gold, he wrote about a hockey player going for gold. He used a story map to plan his work.

First, Cooper chose a setting for his story. It was an ice-hockey game, so it took place at an arena. Then he added a main character and other minor characters. Next, Cooper divided the **plot** of his story into main events. Finally, he planned the outcome of his story.

Setting: Ice rink, a few seconds left in the game

Main character: Jeremy

Minor characters: goalie, fans, defensive players

Plot: The game is tied, with only a few seconds left

Event 1: Jeremy gets the puck.

Event 2: He carries it down the ice.

Event 3: He skates around the defense.

Event 4: He shoots the puck.

Event 5: It hits the post... and bounces in!

Outcome: The Sharks win the game!

Once Cooper had planned his story, he added some similes to bring it to life. The arena was freezing cold. He could say it felt like winter, or he could say it was as icy as a freezer. He could even say it was as cold as ice! You have many choices when you write similes. The words you choose will show the reader your **voice**. Voice is the unique personality of each writer.

Cooper wrote a winning hockey story. He scored big points for using lots of similes. Can you spot them all? How do they set the mood and help bring the story to life?

There were only ten seconds left on the clock. The Sharks were tied with the Bears. Who would take home the gold? Jeremy stole the puck for the Sharks. He blazed down the ice like a comet. But time was running out! The rink was as cold as winter, but his palms were dripping like ice cream on a hot summer day. Jeremy skated past the defenders like they were pylons. Then he shot the puck. It hit the post and clanged as loudly as a bell at recess. The puck bounced past the goalie and into the net. The fans roared like lions. The Sharks had won!

NOW IT'S YOUR TURN!

Now it's your turn to take a shot at it! Use a story map to plan your work. Does your story take place at school or at a circus? Does your main character have freckles or curly hair? Plan your plot details. Then add some similes to spice it up. Paint a picture with words and be a simile superstar!

USING SIMILES IN NONFICTION

You have seen that similes bring fictional stories to life. Similes also make **nonfiction** books more exciting. Nonfiction is writing based on facts, real people, and real events.

The paragraph below is from a book of short **biographies**. A biography is a type of nonfiction book. It is the true story of someone's life. During the American Revolution, Paul Revere was a patriot who wanted the United States to be independent from England. He rode through the night to warn other patriots that the British army was coming. This paragraph describes part of his famous midnight ride.

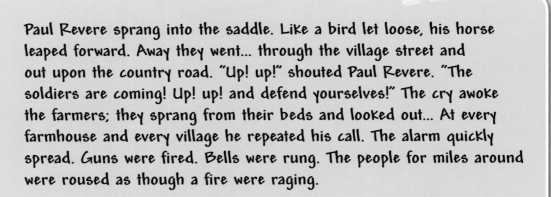

Paul Revere sprang into the saddle. Like a bird let loose, his horse leaped forward. Away they went... through the village street and out upon the country road. "Up! up!" shouted Paul Revere. "The soldiers are coming! Up! up! and defend yourselves!" The cry awoke the farmers; they sprang from their beds and looked out... At every farmhouse and every village he repeated his call. The alarm quickly spread. Guns were fired. Bells were rung. The people for miles around were roused as though a fire were raging.

—Excerpt from *Fifty Famous People*, written by James Baldwin

FIGURE *IT OUT!*

The similes in this passage help bring history to life. You can picture Paul Revere jumping onto his horse and charging down a dirt road. The writer compares the horse leaping forward to "a bird let loose." You can imagine a bird flying quickly out of its cage. It would not wait around for someone to close the cage door! That is how fast Paul Revere set off that night.

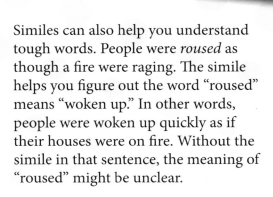

The simile paints a vivid picture for the reader. It also helps create a sense of urgency. Paul Revere sprang into the saddle. His horse charged away like an escaping bird. There was no time to lose! The British were coming! The urgency continues in the second simile of the passage. For miles around, people "were roused as though a fire were raging." You can imagine the panic of a village on fire. People would be shouting and rushing to safety. The similes help you understand the mood along Paul Revere's route.

Similes can also help you understand tough words. People were *roused* as though a fire were raging. The simile helps you figure out the word "roused" means "woken up." In other words, people were woken up quickly as if their houses were on fire. Without the simile in that sentence, the meaning of "roused" might be unclear.

Charlotte wanted to write some exciting nonfiction, too. She decided to write a short **autobiography**. An autobiography is a true story you write about yourself. It is a real account of something that has happened to you.

Charlotte thought about some exciting moments in her life, such as when she moved to a new house, hit a home run, and won a spelling bee. She also fell out of a tree once and broke her arm! In the end, Charlotte decided to write about getting her new puppy. She used a flow chart to write down the events in the order they happened that day.

TOPIC: Picking my puppy!

I woke up early.

We drove to the farm.

I saw the puppies.

One puppy ran over to me.

He licked my face and looked up at me.

I picked him!

Charlotte used her flow chart to write her autobiography. She included as many details as she could remember. Then she added some similes to tell her puppy tale.

I was so excited to get my new puppy! I woke up as early as a bird that day. We drove out to the farm to get my puppy. I bounced up and down on my seat the whole way there! There were five puppies in the litter. Each one was as cute as a button. One puppy ran over and licked my face. His little tongue was rough. His fur was as soft as a sweater. He looked up at me with his big brown eyes. I knew I had just met my best friend.

NOW IT'S YOUR TURN!

Now it's your turn to get real! Think of a true event. Use a flow chart to write down what happened. Then write a paragraph describing the event. Include as many details as you can. And don't forget the similes! They will make your real-life story as large as life.

In the next chapter, you will see how other students helped Charlotte revise her work.

You have learned how to write some super similes. You brainstormed ideas and wrote your first draft. Now you will learn how to revise and edit your work. Use this handy checklist to make sure your similes are as right as rain.

SIMILE REVISION CHECKLIST

1. Does your simile compare two unlike things?

2. Does it use the words "like" or "as" to make the comparison?

3. Does your simile use the five senses?

4. Does it help paint a picture for the reader?

WORK TOGETHER

One way to revise your work is to ask other students to read it. They will tell you if your similes make sense. Can they imagine the pictures you are trying to paint? Is your work creative and interesting? Or do you need to spice up your similes? The group can also help you edit your work. They might spot spelling, grammar, and punctuation errors you missed.

AVOID CLICHÉS

Try to avoid using **clichés**. Clichés are phrases that are used too much and often lose their meaning. For example, "right as rain" means you feel fine. People say it a lot, but it does not create a vivid picture. Can you write a better simile that means you are well?

MAKE IT BETTER

Charlotte shared her autobiography with some other students. They liked her puppy tale, but suggested some ways to improve it.

Jacob thought she should change the word "bird" to "rooster." He lived on a farm and knew that roosters were always up early. Ella told her that "cute as a button" was a cliché. Could she change it to something else? Madison suggested adding some words to the sweater simile to make it more descriptive. Cooper thought she should add some more similes to the paragraph. Maybe she could describe how she bounced in the car and how the puppy's tongue felt.

Charlotte listened carefully to all their suggestions. She agreed that the changes would improve her work. So, she revised it to make it better. You can do it, too! Share your work with other students. They will help you perfect your poetry and prose.

I was so excited to get my new puppy! I woke up as early as a rooster that day. We drove out to the farm to get my puppy. I bounced up and down like a pogo stick the whole way there! There were five puppies in the litter. Each one was cuter than the next. One puppy ran over and licked my face. His little tongue felt like sandpaper. His fur was as soft as a fuzzy brown sweater. He looked up at me with his big brown eyes. I knew I had just met my best friend.

PUBLISHING YOUR SIMILES

Once you have revised and edited your work, it is time to share it! Publishing is the last step in the writing process. Publishing means getting your work ready for an **audience**. An audience is all the people who read or hear what you wrote.

There are lots of ways to publish your work. Give a poem to someone you love. Sing some silly simile songs. Make a book of fairy tales and read it to your little brother. Write a novel and publish it online.

You can publish your nonfiction work, too. Make a memory book and give it to your family. Keep a journal and record what happens to you every day. No matter what you publish, you will feel as proud as a peacock when you share your work!

LEARNING MORE

BOOKS

Muddy as a Duck Puddle and Other American Similes by Laurie Lawlor. Holiday House, 2011.

Similes and Metaphors by Kara Murray. Powerkids Press, 2015.

Stubborn as a Mule and Other Silly Similes by Nancy Loewen. Picture Window Books, 2011.

WEBSITES

Similes Quiz
www.softschools.com/quizzes/grammar/similes/quiz3468.html
Choose the right word to finish the similes in 15 questions.

Kids Educational Games
www.youtube.com/watch?v=XTSCSSHqH_U
Follow this link to watch a video about similes and play an Enchanted Buckets game.

Super Similes Game
www.english-online.org.uk/games/similiframe.htm
Try your luck with this Super Similes slot-machine game.

GLOSSARY

Note: Some boldfaced words are defined where they appear in the book.

audience The people who read or hear your work

autobiography A story of a real person's life, written by that person

biography A story of a real person's life, written by someone else

brainstorm To think of many ideas, often in a group

character A person in a novel, short story, or play

cliché A phrase or saying that is used often

draft A version of something you make before the final copy

figures of speech Words or phrases that are not used in the usual or literal way

graphic organizer A map or diagram that helps organize information in a visual way

hyperbole A figure of speech that exaggerates something to make a point

mood The tone of a story that makes the reader feel a certain way

narrator Someone who tells a story

plot The main events of a story

setting Where and when a story takes place

tension A feeling of nervousness or fear

INDEX